Democracy

for Birds

Eric Thompson began writing comic verse at primary school in Coatbridge and continued the endeavour into the Royal Navy where, as a Scot, he soon found himself being asked to perform at Burns Suppers. From this, he developed his poetry for after dinner entertainment.

A submariner by profession, he is one of the few poets to have written and performed underwater - and probably the only one to have exchanged business letters with an Admiral in verse. He is now much in demand both for after dinner speaking and for live performance of his comic tales.

On leaving the Navy, he entered local politics, an experience which has equipped him to write 'Democracy for Birds' with some authority.

In 1996 he was awarded the BBC Radio Scotland Burns Bicentenary poetry prize for his hilarious parody, 'Ally Shanter', which he also performed at the first Glasgow International Comedy Festival in 2003. It was being invited to write a commemorative poem to mark the bicentenary of his home town of Helensburgh which prompted him to publish his first collection, 'Colquhounsville-sur-Mer'. 'Democracy for Birds' is his second published collection

ERIC THOMPSON

Democracy for Birds

Camis Eskan Publishing

First published in Great Britain in 2004 by Camis Eskan Publishing,
North Lodge, Camis Eskan, Helensburgh, UK, G84 7JZ

Text copyright © Eric Thompson 2004
Illustrations copyright © Eric Thompson 2004
Cover design by Maddy Thompson

A CIP catalogue record for this book is available from the British Library

ISBN 0–9546508–1–6

Printed in Great Britain by Burns Morrison Print Management, 203 Hope Street, Glasgow, G2 UW

Contents

Paradise Lost   1

Albert the Albatross   3

Miner Bird   10

Assertiveness for Ducks   11

Minutes of the Bass Rock Tenants and Residents Association   12

Doves of War   21

Bat in the Belfry   25

On the Edge   26

The Icarus Version   27

Requiescat   28

Outlook Poor   30

Tunnel Vision   31

The Rise and Fall of Chick McLick   33

Jailbird   44

Management Efficiency for Ducks   50

Persecution Complex   51

Notes

'Albert the Albatross' was first performed in 1999 in Edinburgh's historic Signet Library at a fundraising dinner in aid of the Scottish Seabird Centre at North Berwick. *'Minutes of the Bass Rock Tenants and Residents Association'* were read at the same dinner in recognition of the fact that CCTV cameras were about to be installed on the Rock for remote bird watching. *'The Rise and Fall of Chick McLick'* was first performed for the third year pupils at the Thomas Muir High School, Bishopriggs, near Glasgow, in 2003. *'Requiescat'* was first published in Quantum Leap in 2004.

The lessons on management and assertiveness for ducks are by Malvinas Duck who served as Staff Duck in the Third Submarine Squadron at Faslane and on the staff of the Flag Officer Submarines at Fleet Headquarters in North London. *'Doves of War'* is based on the use of carrier pigeons by British submarines during World War 1. (In August 1915, submarine E6 launched four pigeons from Heligoland Bight with an enemy report. The coded message was received at Naval headquarters in Harwich 11.5 hours later, a distance of 140 miles. When submarine C12 tried the same system, the birds had been too well fed and would not leave the submarine!)

'Bat in the Belfry' is derived from the author's study of bats as a possible model for homing torpedoes.

PARADISE LOST

The dodo was a flightless bird.
It saw no need to fly.
It thought there were no predators
But never wondered why.

It lived upon an isle remote
Where species never fought.
So contemplating enemies,
Was never worth the thought.

It had a pair of feathered wings,
Kind Mother Nature's gift,
But as they'd never had a flap,
They'd lost the power to lift.

The dodo foraged on the ground,
And ate till it was fat
But then some hungry sailors came
And that, of course, was that.

Some Notes on the Albatross

……….. The Dodo is not the only bird to have been reduced to extinction by human hand. Today, long line fishermen are decimating albatross numbers.

With wingspans in excess of three metres, the albatross glides above the southern oceans for years on end, returning to land only for mating. Why, after years at sea, this solitary creature should decide to return to dry land remains one of nature's great mysteries.

Albert the Albatross

Part 1 - Serenity

Albert was an albatross.
A solo life led he.
He glided silent on the wind
Above the restless sea.

Albert was serene and led
A very tranquil life.
For Albert was a bachelor
And did not have a wife.

But after seven years at sea
His hormones gave a surge
And in between his tucked-up legs
He felt a strange new urge.

His streamlined shape became deformed
His stalling speed was dropping.
Then all around his landing gear
His feathers started popping.

Part 2 - Panic

Albert lowered his beak
On his neck long and sleek,
And he gazed in alarm at his rear.
For this threatened his flight
And was costing him height
And it looked aeronautically queer.

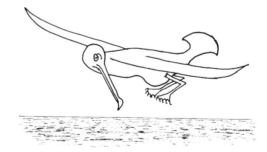

In his albatross way,
He called out, 'Mayday!'
And reported a technical hitch.
For his feathers were loose
And he flew like a goose
And his crutch was consumed with an itch.

Albert saw distant sand,
On which he could land
And signalled his incoming number.
Then lowered his feet
Which were tucked-up so neat
And unfolded his legs from their slumber.

Now, an albatross white
Is majestic in flight.
It's a truly magnificent bird.
But its landing technique
Is an absolute freak
And, more often than not, quite absurd.

As he came screaming down
With his face in a frown
And his beak all prepared for the thump,
At the front of his mind
Was what followed behind
And the fear that he'd land on his lump.

From what's known as a stall
Albert entered freefall
With his wings arching out as a brake.
Then his feet hit the beach
With a web ripping screech
And he knew he had made a mistake.

For his tail was too high
Which had lowered his thigh,
And his legs were too short for his lump.
So his balls bit the dust
Which switched braking to thrust
As he fought to gain height at his rump.

With his tail in the air
And his eyes in wide stare
And his beak heading straight for the sand.
Albert braced for a bit
Then went arse over tit
Did three somersaults then failed to stand.

Part 3 – Courtship

'That landing's a mess,'
Said the young albatress
Who had watched Albert hitting the deck.
'If you're here for a date
'With the prospect to mate
'There's no way I'm going out with a wreck!'

But her knees went quite weak
At the size of his beak
And she drooled at his masculine feature.
Then softly she said,
'Though I'm no good in bed,
'I'd be willing if you'll be my teacher.'

Albert straightened his wing
For this chick wore no ring,
And he strutted his stuff to impress her.
Then into his mind
Came the swelling behind
And the fear that his lump would distress her.

'Though I think I'm in love,'
He cooed like a dove.
'I regret I'm just down from the sky.
'And unable to jump
'On account of a lump.'
But she said, 'Just let's give it a try.'

Part 4 - Bliss

Now Albert is an albatross.
A married man is he.
He's got a nest in which to rest
And never goes to sea.

Miner Bird

I am a pit canary.
A miner bird am I.
They send me down the mineshafts first
So miner lads won't die.
And if I sniff some poisonous gas,
My job is to collapse,
And fall like dead from off my perch
To warn the other chaps.

They never doubt my actions.
The Union has less clout.
For when I'm bored I fake a swoon
And get the men all out.

ASSERTIVENESS FOR DUCKS

1. Identify equal opportunity.

2. Investigate.

3. Make your move.

4. Sit Tight.

………. and then there are those difficult public meetings.

Minutes of the Forty Third Extraordinary General Meeting of the Bass Rock Tenants and Residents Association

The Chairman welcomed members to the meeting and apologized for calling it during the mating season which had been due to unforeseen circumstances. Bill Gannet, representing the Federation of Long Range Diving Birds, said that there was nothing unforeseen about the mating season. It had been in his diary since last year and all his members were back for it. Janet Gannet observed that whilst his members might be back for it, they were a month late and so was she.

The Chairman explained that it had been the circumstances of the meeting and not the mating season which had been unforeseen, the circumstances being the recent appearance of CCTV cameras on the Rock.

Jill Guillemot of the Mother's Union said that as far as her members were concerned, the mating season was over but the Reverend Donald Mallard of the United Free Ducks disagreed. He was appalled by the amount of recreational mating taking place. Couples co-habiting without the intent to rear chicks, he said, should be refused nesting space as many young couples in his parish were expecting their first egg and were still nestless. Sir

John Cormorant of the Old Shags Association said that the real cause of the problem was gay nesting and he proposed that all gay birds should be sent to Rockall. The Chairman reminded members that he had called the meeting to address the CCTV issue and did not wish to be drawn down any gay rabbit holes. Sir John added that the Chairman would be hard pressed to find any gay rabbits on Rockall.

Mrs. Gemma Gull of the Woman's Offshore Institute was fully in support of the Reverend Mallard and drew the committee's attention to the number of single females who had been laying eggs purely to jump the nesting queue. In agreeing, Father Frank Avocet, a Black-tailed Godwit, said that his flock were all wading birds and he was already losing too many of them in the deep water off the rock. He regarded affordable seafront nesting sites as his highest priority.

Mrs. Edith Eider of Ducks Against Scandinavian Quilts said that her top priority was predatory quilters. They were getting her down….and no pun was intended. She called for a campaign of positive action. Fennella Sanderling of the Unwinged Society complained that she had been perched on the foghorn when it went off and was now deaf. She called for it to be switched-off during roosting hours. The Chairman replied that he had been unable to hear Miss Sanderling as the foghorn had been sounding but pointed-out that the meeting had been called to address the CCTV issue and not the foghorn. He called for the Secretary to read the minutes of the previous meeting.

The Secretary reported that no minutes had been taken at the previous meeting as the previous meeting had passed a motion banning the use of quills. She tendered apologies from Jock-the-Auk who had flown to Edinburgh for the Scottish Independent Seabirds conference. The Reverend Mallard wished to know why the meeting had been called on the Sabbath day. This, the Secretary explained, was because February had 29 days. The Chairman then moved to the main item on the agenda which was the sudden appearance of CCTV cameras on the Rock.

Kitty Wake of St Haddock's Sunday School also agreed with the Reverend Mallard. Christ may have loved fishermen but gangs of young razorbills mating in full view of her chicks was downright anti-social. She called for a complete ban on mating after the first eggs were hatched. Trevor Tern of the Senior Citizens Group disagreed as many of his members would have difficulty completing their courting rituals before the first chicks were hatched. Willie Seagull of the Cleansing Department had read in a fish-and-chip paper in North Berwick that there was a new drug called Niagara which removed the need for lengthy courtship rituals. He proposed that stocks should be held on the Rock. The Chairman ruled the matter outside the scope of the meeting and returned to the subject of the CCTV. Trevor Tern said that one of his members had already tried the drug and was unable to land until the effects had worn-off.

As a supplementary question, Mr. Seagull asked if the new television equipment would be able to receive Sky Sports as he worked on Saturday afternoons. The Chairman thought this unlikely. Hughie Skua who had recently been elected as Chair of the Heart of Midlothian 'Sack the Board' Campaign said that watching live football was a complete waste of time nowadays as the roofs on the new all-weather stadia made it impossible to bomb the visiting supporters. There was more fun to be had bombing cars in supermarket car parks.

Jill Guillemot asked if the new television equipment could be used as a video link to the new Scottish Parliament. Hughie Skua replied that the new Scottish Parliament was a complete waste of money and he could not wait to crap on its roof. The Chairman thanked Mr Skua for his advice but felt that it lacked relevance to the agenda item. It was his belief that the cameras could only be accessed by people on the mainland who wished to intrude on the privacy of Rock residents.

Councillor Sheila Shearwater, Crag Central (Conservative), said that her constituents were outraged by CCTV cameras in their neighbourhood as this would reduce the value of their nests. She had been in touch with the Scottish Offshore Rock Afforestation Society which had the acronym SORAS. They were willing to plant trees to restore privacy.

Councillor Ellen Osprey, Crag North (Liberal Democrat), said that SORAS was a pain in the butt. She had been in touch with the Scottish Offshore Defoliation Society which had the acronym SODS and they were completely opposed to all unnatural arborial cultivation on offshore rocks as it would attract crows and Conservatives.

On a point of order, Fanny Fulmar complained that Sharon Shag was having a fish during the meeting which was in breach of the constitution. Standing Order 23 stated very clearly that members wishing to have a fish had to leave the meeting. Ms Shag said that it was Ms Fulmar who was out of order. The 'no fish eating' rule did not apply as she had swallowed her fish before the meeting and

was merely regurgitating it. She said that in future Ms Fulmar should address her by her proper name which was Phalacrocorax Aristotelis and not Sharon. She also pointed out that Phil Puffin had been sitting with four fish in his beak since the meeting began.

The Chairman asked Mr.Puffin to explain his conduct but Mr.Puffin declined to reply. Bill Gannet, speaking on behalf of Mr.Puffin, considered it unreasonable to ask Mr Puffin to speak when it was obvious that he had four fish in his beak. Mr.Puffin, he said, was in a Catch 22 situation. He could not speak because he had fish in his beak and he could not eat them because of Standing Order 23. The Chairman then returned to the main item on the agenda which was the installation of CCTV equipment on the Rock.

Phalacrocorix Aristotelix Shag thought that puffins had fantastically colourful beaks and wanted to know what they used for make-up. The Reverend Mallard said that puffins' beaks were sexually provocative and called for them to wear hoods in public.

The Chairman agreed that puffins did have unusually colourful beaks but emphasised that the meeting had been convened to discuss the CCTV cameras. Sir John Cormorant said that has far as he was concerned, all puffins were gay and should be sent to Rockall.

Councillor Shearwater said that apart from the issue of nest prices, the Rock was not fit to be seen on television as successive Councils had let it run down. She proposed that it be re-guanoed before any filming began. Jill Guillemot agreed and suggested that dayglow orange would really put the Rock on the tourist map. The Chairman ruled her motion incompetent as no seabirds could deliver dayglow orange guano. Rab Oystercatcher of Seafront Decorations Ltd disagreed. Whilst accepting that it would not be possible on a diet of oysters, he was confident that he could deliver if he switched his employees to moules marinieres. His company would wish to bid for the contract. The Secretary pointed out that if his company wished to bid for the contract, Mr. Oystercatcher would have a conflict of interest and should withdraw from the meeting.

A scuffle ensued over a fish dropped by Phil Puffin and the Chairman ordered Hughie Skua to leave the meeting for spitting. Mr Skua then spat at the Chairman and left the meeting.

The Chairman then called for a vote on the motion that 'CCTV equipment should be banned from the Bass Rock'. The motion was defeated by 1.3 million votes to five, Bill Gannet casting his block vote against.

The Chairman thanked members for attending and closed the meeting.

During the First World War, British submarines used homing pigeons to carry vital information back to base when beyond radio range. The system worked but was not without technical hitches ....

Doves of War

'Up periscope,' the Captain roared
And up the lookstick flew.
He snatched a fifteen second look
Then turned to face his crew.

'The target is within our sights.
'We need to signal back
'And let the Admiralty know
'We're ready to attack.'
'Signalman, write that down in code
'And fetch our feathered ace.
'Then tie my signal to his leg
'And send him back to base.'

The submarine rose from the sea
Like prehistoric beast.
Its conning tower was opened quick.
The pigeon was released.
Arooga – Arooga – Arooga,
The klaxon sounded thrice,
And to the deep the boat returned,
Its crew as cool as ice.

'The target's coming at us,'
Roared the Captain with delight,
And hugged the slim brass periscope
To keep it in his sight.
'Good God!' he groaned with tortured look.
'This is a bloody farce!
'Our pigeon's landed on my 'scope.
'And all I see's its arse!'

'A pigeon's not a seabird, sir,'
The First Lieutenant said.
'It cannot land upon the waves
'And simply used its head.'

And every time the 'scope went down,
The bird flew round in search.
And every time the 'scope went up,
It landed on its perch.
'Good God,' the angry Captain cried.
'How am I to attack
'When every time I raise my 'scope,
'That bloody pigeon's back?'

'Perhaps,' the First Lieutenant said,
'He's waiting for his mate.
'She's nesting in the engine room
'Inside a piston crate.'

'Well get her out!'
The Captain roared.
'Prepare the hen for flight.
'And get the pair both on their way
'So I can have my sight!'

'I'm sorry, sir,' a stoker said,
'The hen has just been fed.
'There's no way now she'll take the air.
'She thinks it's time for bed!'

'God give me strength!' the Captain roared.
'To fly is what they're for!
'Has no one told our pigeons that
'This country is at war?'

'I think,' the First Lieutenant said,
'To press home your attack.
'We'll have to surface one more time
'And get our pigeon back!'

Bats are neither birds nor blind but they do navigate in the dark using sound rather than sight. In familiar surroundings, however, they navigate by memory……. which is fine until someone puts a new obstacle in their way.

Bat in the Belfry

The little bat flew out at night
To navigate by pinging.
It flew into the new church bell
Which left its ears a-ringing.

On the Edge

Today I learn to fly. Yes,sir!
Just one more strip of rabbit
Then it's over the edge.
Mum brought it in for breakfast.
She said, 'Tomorrow, you catch your own!'
- That's after I've learned to fly, of course.
Been practising for weeks.
Just standing on the edge
Flexing the old wings.
Almost getting lift-off without even trying.
All I have to do now is step out.
My wings will do the rest.
No bother at all!
Just one strip of rabbit
Then I'm off. Yes,sir!
- Actually, Dad will be home soon.
So I'll just wait for him.
- In fact, I'll just learn to fly
Tomorrow.

Man has also tried to fly. Daedalus made wings so that he and his son, Icarus, could escape imprisonment but, according to Greek legend, Icarus ignored his father's wise advice and flew too close to the sun causing the wax to melt and his wings to disintegrate. The son's version is somewhat different.

The Icarus Version

Daedalus, the cunning man,
Made wings of wax and feather,
And leapt out from his prison wall
Connected up with leather.
When high aloft, the wax went soft,
Then melted altogether.
So Daedalus plunged to the sea
And cursed the sunny weather.

Icarus, his son, looked out
And watched his father's folly.
He said, 'This just confirms for me,
'My old man's off his trolley.'

Requiescat

Allsorts licked his paw and thought that rabbit tasted nice.
In gastronomic merit it was streets ahead of mice.
In fact, if cats had menus, there's no doubt that he would choose
A rabbit for his breakfast just before the morning snooze.

Oh, that vital morning snooze which every working cat requires
For analysing hunting and to fantasize desires,
But the problem is the ears. They simply never go to sleep.
They keep sucking-in the noises, every bark and little cheep.
All that barking from the canines which the cat regards as thick
And the chirping of the birds whose feathers always make him sick,
But a feline can't ignore them for it's always on its guard.
Even when its eyes are resting, it's condemned to listen hard.

First the bees all buzz with rapture whilst commuting from their hive.
Then the milkman and the postman and the digger all arrive,
And the children and the buses and the traffic on the road,
And the telephone and radio then light bulbs which explode.
How, one asks, can cats find peace to have that vital morning nap
When their private feline hear-space is so crammed with sonic scrap?

Allsorts had his morning snooze in this cacophony of sound
And he dreamt of being a rabbit with his bedroom underground.

OUTLOOK POOR

I spy with my little eye,
A kestrel hovering in the sky.
I may be wrong but have a hunch,
It plans to have me for its lunch.

TUNNEL VISION

An ostrich hiding on the plane,
Its head deep in the sand,
Was ravished by a vulture
Which was rather underhand.

Chicken Licken Re-visited

When the legendary Chicken Licken was playing under a tree, a nut fell on his head and, thinking that the sky was falling down, he rushed-off to tell the king and on the way he met Henny Penny, Cocky Locky, Ducky Lucky, Drakey Lakey, Goosie Lucy, Turkey Lurkey and Foxy Loxy and they all joined him in his mission to tell the king. The tale has been read to generations of children but what relevance does it have to the chickens of today growing up in socially disadvantaged council housing estates in suburban Scotland?..............

The Rise and Fall of Chick McLick

Wee Chick McLick was busy spraying graffiti on the school wall when a nut fell out of a tree and hit him on the head.

'Eff off!' he cried, waving two fingers up the street. 'Ah'm gettin' the polis to you.'

So Chick McLick rushed away to get the police and on the way he met Jen the Hen.
'How'sit going Hen?' he asked.
'Fine, son,' replied Jen the Hen. 'How's yersel'?'
'No fine!' said Chick McLick. 'Some eejit just hit me on the heid and ah'm away tae get the polis.'
'That's not on, son,' said Jen the Hen. 'Ah'm coming with you.'

So Chick McLick and Jen the Hen set off to find the police and on the way met Big Jock the Cock.

'Whit's the game, Wee Man?' asked Big Jock.

'Some effin' eejit just hit me ower the heid wi' a bottle, Big Man, and am away tae get the polis.'

'Wastin' your time, son. There's nae polis up here these days. You'll have tae go tae oor local Cooncillor and complain aboot a breakdoon in law and order.'

So Chick McLick, Jen the Hen and Big Jock the Cock set off to complain to their local Councillor and on the way they met Ducky McLuckie.

'Haw, Duckie,' cried Chick McLick. 'Some eejit just split ma effin' heid wide open wi' a bottle and we're away tae see oor local Cooncillor tae demand protection.'

'Basic human right that,' said Duckie McLuckie, 'but your wastin' your time goin' tae the local Cooncillor. He's too busy doin' deals wi' Donald the Developer tae put hooses on the Greenbelt. You'll need tae see oor MSP.'

So Chick McLick, Jen the Hen, Big Jock the Cock and Ducky McLuckie set off to see their MSP and on the way they met Jake the Drake.

'Where are youse all goin' tae?' asked Jake the Drake with great suspicion.

'Tae see oor MSP,' replied Chick McLick with great authority. 'Some effin' eejit's just smashed ma heid wide open and ma brains is fallin' oot! We're aff tae demand protection.'

'Wasting your time, so you are,' said Jake the Drake. 'Oor MSP's in the opposition. Ye'll need tae form a pressure group and lobby the Minister of Justice at the Scottish Parliament.'

So Chick McLick, Jen the Hen, Big Jock the Cock, Ducky McLuckie and Jake the Drake, set off for Edinburgh to lobby the Minister of Justice, and on the way they met Juicy Goosie.

'Hello there boys,' said Juicy Goosie, adjusting her boob tube. 'Is there anything I can do for you the day?'

'Aye,' replied Chick McLick. 'You can join ma protest group because some gang o' eejits just ripped ma skull wide open and we're aff tae see the Minister of Justice tae demand protection.'

'Nice one, Chick ma boy,' said Juicy Goosie, 'but there's nae point in seeing him. He's a Literal Democrat. He's only coalescent. You'll need tae see the First Minister. He's Born Again Labour. He's the one wi' all the power.'

So Chick McLick, Jen the Hen, Big Jock the Cock, Ducky McLuckie, Jake the Drake, and Juicy Goosie set off for Edinburgh to see the First Minister, and on the way they met Turk McGurk.

'Hu-Hu-Hu-Hullorer,' gobbled Turk McGurk nervously as they approached. 'Ur y-youse the new gang up here?'

'No way, Turk,' replied Chick McLick. 'We're a pressure group! We're goin' tae Edinburgh tae see the First Minister tae demand protection frae that gang o' eejits that just claimed oor streets.'

'N-N-Nae point in that, lads,' stuttered Turk McGurk. 'He's B-Born again Labour. He takes all his instructions frae the P-P-Party Headquarters in London. If youse want tae r-reclaim the streets, it'll need to be in the Q-Q-Queen's Speech, s-s-so it will.

You'll need tae go and see the Prime Minister at Westminster. He's one of us.'
'Whit?' exclaimed Chick McLick. 'The Prime Minister's a turkey?'
'N-N-Naw!' gulped Turk McGurk. 'Ah meant he's U-U-Unborn Again.'

So Chick McLick, Jen the Hen, Big Jock the Cock, Ducky McLuckie, Jake the Drake, Juicy Goosie and Turk McGurk set off for London to demand protection from the Prime Minister, and on the way they met Poxy Foxy.
'What's up, my friends?' asked Poxy Foxy with great concern.
'Not effin' much,' cried Chick McLick. 'Ah was just nearly killed by a gang o' eejits wi' knives and bottles and we're aff tae tell the Prime Minister that law and order has completely broke doon in oor estate He's goin' tae put it in the Queen's speech.'

'Wasting your time, my friends,' said Poxy Foxy. 'That Prime Minister's all spin and no substance. He said he would be tough on crime five years ago and look what's just happened to you. See they politicians - all talk and no action!
It's enough to make you spit! So, my friends, why don't you all just come home with me and I'll fix you up with something to make you feel better?'

So Chick McLick, Jen the Hen, Big Jock the Cock, Ducky McLuckie, Jake the Drake, Juicy Goosie and Turk McGurk all went off to Poxy Foxy's house and he gave them each four temazipan and a snort of coke.

'Oh yes,' cried Chick McLick, 'this is the stuff! Now ma heid doesnae hurt any more. Gonnae gie us some more o'that, Poxy?'

'You, my young friend, can have as much of that as you like,' said Poxy Foxy. 'Plenty more where that came from .... but you all owe me fifty quid for this lot and it'll be fifty quid up front for the next lot. OK?..... and, by the way, the last punter who didnae pay got his head split open.'

So Chick McLick, Jen the Hen, Big Jock the Cock, Ducky McLuckie, Jake the Drake, Juicy Goosie and Turk McGurk all went back home to raise a hundred quid and on the way they broke into Billy the Budgie's cage and nicked his Playstation. Then they mugged wee Hammy the Hamster who was busy spraying graffiti on the school wall.

Eff Off!' cried Hammy the Hamster, waving two fingers after them. 'Ah'm goin' tae get the polis to you.'

JAILBIRD

The court rose. The judge swept in,
Lord Justice Tawny Owl,
In regal splendour on the bench.
A case of murder fowl.

He preened his wig. He flapped his gown
He scanned the hoi polloi.
Then from the dock, a voice rang out,
'Well, who's a pretty boy?'

Lord Justice Owl with angered scowl
Called, 'Silence in my court!'
Then loud the order echoed back.
'Yes. Silence in my court!'

In the dock a parrot perched
With chain clamped round its claw,
And when Judge Owl required its name
It squawked back 'Mick Macaw.'

44

The charge was read. A chick was dead.
Macaw now stood accused,
And, balanced on one shackled leg,
He winked and looked amused.

The prosecuting counsel swooped,
A famous legal eagle.
'That parrot killed the chick, my Lord.
'Both evil and illegal.'

Defence counsel raised his beak,
A fairly humble seagull.
'The chick had led my client astray.
'Her game was to inveigle.'

'Objection!' screeched the eagle.
'The chick was pure as snow.
'Macaw has mugged a chick before.
This time, he's got to go.'

45

'I'm innocent!' Macaw proclaimed.
'And this is pure damn cheek,
'To have an honest bird like me
'Hauled up before the beak!'

The jury, twelve good crows and true,
Withdrew in equanimity
And, on return, their verdict gave
Achieved with unanimity.

'Birds of the jury,' asked Judge Owl,
 'What verdict do you draw?'
'Not guilty,' came the fateful cry.
(The voice came from Macaw).

'Not guilty, did I hear you say?
'You crows must be half-witted!
'This means the case must be dismissed.
'Macaw will be acquitted!'

'Objection, 'cried the eagle,
'Most serious legal flaw!'
'Impersonating juries
'Is in breach of statute law!'

Macaw's beak smashed the dock,
His temper on display,
And screaming 'vulture' at the judge,
He ripped the sill away.

'Guilty as charged,' the eagle roared.
'Guilty,' cawed the crows.
'I find you guilty,' cried the judge,
'As your behaviour shows.'

Lord Justice Owl from lofty bench
With grave judicial blink,
Pronounced the sentence on Macaw,
Full fifteen years in clink.

Defence in mitigation pled
From jail he be excused.
Macaw, they claimed, was victim too.
When young he was abused.

      With raven warder at each side
      To escort him to cells,
      Macaw then thanked the jury with
      Some choice expletive yells.

            He turned his venom on the bench.
            'Your Honour is half plastered!
            'Your parents never laid your egg.
            'You are a cuckoo's bastard!'

                  Macaw in chains was led away
                  To cries of public joy.
                  Then from the bench a voice rang out,
                  'Well, who's a naughty boy?'

MANAGEMENT EFFICIENCY FOR DUCKS

.... An efficient duck

.... maintains a clear desk!

PERSECUTION COMPLEX

I have a chip on my shoulder.

   - Not because I'm ethnic minority,
    Or victim of prejudice,
    Or woman starved of equal opportunity.
  - No, because it was dropped by a passing seagull.

But why me, O Lord, why me?

By the same author

COLQUHOUNSVILLE-SUR-MER (ISBN 0-9546508-0-8)

A collection of comic narrative verse about events, true and apocryphal, in the upper reaches of the River Clyde including 'Noah's Comet', 'A Wife, a Yacht and a Bottle of Gin' and 'The Helensburgh Bicentenary'. Illustrated by the author.

LOVE SONGS FOR THE ROMANTICALLY CHALLENGED (ISBN 0-9546508-2-4)

The perfect antidote for romantic slush. A tonic for all those who understand that love in the real world is rarely shrouded in wine and roses. (Due for publication January 2005).

Published by:

Camis Eskan Publishing
North Lodge
Camis Eskan
Helensburgh
Scotland
G84 7JZ

tel/fax 01436 678943
eric@camiseskan1.demon.co.uk

Gannets outgrow colonies to buck trend in falling seabird numbers

The Herald
Tuesday September 14, 2004

THE population of gannets has grown significantly over the past 10 years, with the birds becoming so overcrowded on traditional nesting sites that they have established a new colony, researchers have said.

The initial results of the first survey for a decade has found that their numbers have continued to grow by around 10% despite the effects of climate change causing a drop in other seabird populations.

One colony – Bass Rock in East Lothian – has grown by 20%, according to Scottish Natural Heritage (SNH), which commissioned the gannets survey.

VICKY COLLINS
ENVIRONMENT
CORRESPONDENT